TRENCH PICTURES

Major W. Redmond at 54. (Feb. 1915).

TRENCH PICTURES FROM FRANCE

BY
MAJOR WILLIAM REDMOND
M.P.

Killed in Action, June 1917

With a Biographical Introduction by
E. M. SMITH-DAMPIER

"Your cause is one, Dark Rosaleen,
 Where I know not wrong from right;
But I know the eyes of a fairy queen,
 And the heart of a gallant knight!"

LONDON: ANDREW MELROSE, LTD.
3 YORK STREET, COVENT GARDEN, W.C.2

First published in August 1917
Reprinted September 1917

FOREWORD

BY MRS. WILLIAM REDMOND

The articles which make up the bulk of this book were contributed to the *Daily Chronicle* under a pseudonym. I have read with real pleasure the Introduction written by Miss Smith-Dampier, which shows a sympathetic understanding of my husband's nature and brings out vividly his personality. I am grateful to Miss Smith-Dampier for her sympathetic work, and to the Editor of the *Daily Chronicle* for the interest he has shown in arranging for the publication of my husband's sketches in book form.

Eleanor Redmond.

Glenbrook, Delgany, Co. Wicklow, Ireland.
July 12, 1917.

CONTENTS

	PAGE
IN MEMORIAM	11
INTRODUCTION	13

CHAPTER

I.	A Garden Trench	35
II.	To Charing Cross via the Red Cross	47
III.	As they Fought, so they Died	65
IV.	The Taking of Ginchy	73
V.	The Camp-Fire Prayer	85
VI.	How the Colonel came Back	95
VII.	In the Darkened Church	105
VIII.	The Frozen Front Line	117
IX.	Religion and the War	127
X.	The Square of Empire	139
XI.	In "No Man's Land"	151
XII.	"Jack," the Pet Dog	161

APPENDIX

MAJOR REDMOND'S LAST SPEECH   173

In Memoriam

W. R.

Oh, Michael stood on the walls of heaven
    And watched the souls come in,
For the hosts of God were up once more
    To harry the hosts of sin.

Michael he took the moon for a shield,
    And a brand of the burning levin,
And flew to earth through the reek of blood
    That hid the stars in heaven.

Michael went down by Weeping Well
    To rest him at eventide,
And he saw there a maiden fair,
    And a dead man lay beside.

Oh, he looked on her with the piercing eye
    That's pure from spot of sin,
And saw right well the hound of hell
    That gnawed her heart within.

And like a cup that's lifted up
    With royal wine a-brim,
Michael, that looked upon the dead,
    Beheld the heart of him.

" Look up, thou daughter of earth, look up,
    Great grace is thine, I wis !
Lovers hast thou had many a one,
    But never a one like this.

IN MEMORIAM

"Oh, well he knew thy deadly sin
  As well he knew thy worth,
For he looked on thee with the eyes of heaven
  And not with the eyes of earth.

"Daughter of earth, now look thou forth,
  And see where the souls of men
Go forth on the night like the wild marsh-fires
  That flicker above the fen.

"And see where the souls of men rise up
  Like stars in heaven to shine!
A jewel set on Our Lady's brow
  Is the soul whose love is thine.

"And lo, the reek of flame and blood,
  Where, like sparks from the nether pit,
The eyes of the ravening hounds of hell
  Drive by on the blast with it!

"Take heed, take heed lest thy foot go down
  Behind the hounds of hell!"
Michael he seized his shining shield,
  And turned him from Weeping Well.

He turned his face to the reeling hosts,
  And brandished the burning levin,
For the quick fought on while the dead looked down
  And watched from the walls of heaven!

                        E. M. SMITH-DAMPIER.

Mr. W. Redmond at 25. (1886).

INTRODUCTION

WILLIE REDMOND

A WITTY, joyous partisan in the most bitter of political controversies, who yet made no personal enemies; a man of middle age who left home and career to train as a soldier; a Catholic who, foreseeing death, embraced it in the hope that his blood would bring healing to his own country—such was the man whose loss has caused a public grief so general and sincere as to surprise even those who loved him best. Other Members of Parliament before Willie Redmond—some ten or eleven—had died for their country in the war, yet not one of these deaths was felt as deeply as his in both Houses. " If Willie could come back," said his widow to me, "he would be so surprised, he would wonder what all the fuss was about." It is in these words that we find the key to the secret. The single eye—utter unselfconsciousness—this is what makes Willie Redmond a typical figure. A thousand men bleed and

INTRODUCTION

die ; only by a rare combination of qualities does an individual stand out as their spiritual representative, summing up in one hero-figure their finest valour, their most unselfish aims. And this romantic, impetuous Irishman combined them all.

William Hoey Kearney Redmond was born in 1861 at Wexford. To those who believe that the pre-natal influence of " that kindly nurse," a particular countryside, may colour a life to its end, it will seem fitting that he should come of a city long associated with his forefathers. The statue of his grand-uncle, John Edward, who in 1859 represented Wexford as Liberal member, stands in Redmond Place, with these words on its pedestal : "My heart is with the City of Wexford. Nothing can extinguish that love but the cold soil of the grave."

It was at Parnell's invitation that John Redmond entered the House of Commons in 1881. William, at that time lieutenant in the City of Wexford Battalion of the Royal Irish Regiment, resigned his commission in order to take part in the Land League movement, and his twenty-first birthday was spent in Kilmainham Gaol.

At the time when " The Invincibles " were

INTRODUCTION

undergoing trial for the Phœnix Park murders, the Redmond brothers were sent by Parnell to Australia, commissioned to raise funds for the Nationalist cause. It was no easy time for such an errand, yet the journey resulted in the addition of £15,000 to the party funds. It was during this expedition that he met and married Miss Dalton, daughter of a prominent Australian magistrate.

William Redmond was nominated as Parnellite candidate for Wexford in 1883, when he beat " The O'Conor Don," a descendant of kings, by three to one. He sat till 1885, when he was returned for County Fermanagh. In September 1888, during Balfour's Secretaryship, he was sentenced under the Crimes Act to three months' imprisonment without hard labour, for inciting to resistance of the sheriff's authority during an eviction at Coolroe. (This, by the by, was a period when political prisoners shared the ordinary severities of prison-life.) " I undoubtedly," said he, " cheered those men when they were defending their homes against unjust eviction, and I shall continue to cheer every man who does so."

Here we have no mere political war-cry, but an expression of human sympathy. This man worked outwards to his political principles

INTRODUCTION

from the fundamentals of human nature. Better than most, he could have stood the sardonic test proposed in *Sartor Resartus*, of appearing without conventional trappings before a naked House of Commons!

When the great " split " rent his party in 1890, William Redmond stood by Parnell. His action made him the object of much partisan hatred, which he took in a thoroughly sporting spirit. Two years later he won East Clare for the Parnellites, and represented that constituency until his death.

In those days, now remote, there was a certain caste prejudice against the Irish members. Thackeray had set the fashion of considering them " no gentlemen," and *Punch* and the *Times* followed his lead. But those who saw Willie Redmond, whatever their prejudice, never failed to recognise that here was an Irish member who was not merely a gentleman, but one whose charming courtesy and dare-devil wit recalled the most picturesque traditions of the eighteenth century. His gifts, at this period, were considered to be less those of the orator than the improvisatore. Outside the House he could move an audience at his will. In S. Stephen's, however, he was content to be overshadowed by his

INTRODUCTION

brother, the leader of the Nationalist Party. His own speciality was the pricking of bubbles—the art of happy interruption.

"For many years," says a personal reminiscence, "Willie was the jester of the House, and the smoking-room was always chuckling over his latest *mot*." Yet he was popular even with those who felt the edge of his wicked wit. "He had"—so runs Mr. Asquith's tribute—"a certain genius of imagination and sympathy which enabled him always to understand the scruples and differences of honest opponents." To this Colonel Lockwood bears witness in quoting Willie Redmond's own words: "You go in what you believe to be the straight path, and I in mine. In the end we shall meet." This fine chivalry—the spirit which led Earl Percy to take the dead Douglas by the hand—is echoed in the saying of his great opponent, Sir Edward Carson: "I had no bitter word with him."

When war broke out in 1914, it troubled no heart more deeply than Willie Redmond's. For a long time, says Mrs. Redmond, he refused so much as to look at a newspaper. "If I'm too old to fight," he said, "at least I will not sit comfortably in an arm-chair and read what other men are doing and suffering." It was

INTRODUCTION

the first Zeppelin raid on England which finally made him take action; if women and children were killed, he would remain a non-combatant no longer. That same winter he joined the Royal Irish Division, raised, chiefly by John Redmond and Devlin, among the Catholics of the West and South. To one of his political principles, the donning of the British uniform was a moral effort; but his keen vision pierced through to the fundamentals of the struggle, and his heart warmed to the larger patriotism.

"There may be a few," were his own words, "who think that Germany would not injure Ireland, and might even benefit her. I hope the Clare people will rely on no such rash statements. If the Germans come here . . . they will be our masters, and we at their mercy. What that mercy is likely to be, judge by the mercy shown to Belgium. I am far too old to be a soldier, but I mean to do my best, for whatever life remains in me, to show that Ireland at least is true to her treaties, and not in any way ungrateful to her friends throughout the world." Again: "No Irishman worth his salt would be beholden for any favour to the men who have ruined Belgium."

Here is an object-lesson for those who believe

INTRODUCTION

that love of Humanity which man hath not seen is necessarily inconsistent with love of the country that he hath seen.

> "How can man die better,
> Than facing fearful odds,
> For the ashes of his fathers,
> And the temples of his gods?"

This is a question to which the superior person who deals in windy generalities has hitherto supplied no effective answer. Because love for his own land lay warm at the heart's core of William Redmond, he was able to perceive that in this war his country's cause was also the world's. If a man loves his mother, is he more likely or less to fight for the help of women in general? This is a point which it seems unnecessary to labour.

His decision came as a surprise, not only to the world at large, but to those who knew him best. "It was not till this epoch in his career," says T. P. O'Connor, "that people—even his most intimate friends—began to realise Willie Redmond. Even then this entry into the Army seemed rather a passing fancy, a transient enthusiasm, than real business."

It soon became apparent that the business was very real. At the Fermoy training-camp

INTRODUCTION

he underwent all the discipline of drill and route-marching which one would imagine peculiarly irksome to a man no longer young, a man not in the best of health, a man who had for many years led a sedentary existence.

" At Fermoy "—I quote by permission from Captain Stephen Gwynn's article in the *Freeman's Journal* of June 19—" the 6th Royal Irish and the Connaught Rangers lay together in the new barracks for many months. That made us a joint mess of some seventy officers, and, among the older men, he and I were almost the only Nationalists. It was a society in which he felt strange, and at the mess he was quiet, reserved, and rather shy. It amused me to find how impossible it was for any of the subalterns to imagine this gentlest of gentlemen as a turbulent leader of revolt. Sometimes I tried to draw him into one of those moods of reminiscence which made him the best company in the House of Commons smoking-room, but I never succeeded. . . . All that his brother officers knew in earlier days was that they loved him. . . . Quite literally; I never heard any one say that he was liked. The other was always the word. The only thing I ever heard said in his dispraise was that he could not bring himself to be hard enough with the men. I dare say that, as a soldier, he had that fault. He lacked the years or decades that should have fitted him at all points for his proper vocation. But a soldier he was by nature ; and it is a happy thing to think that he enjoyed for its own sake the life into which he came thus out of due time. . . . He was made for the simple life of disciplined obedience and utter loyalty which is the soldier's ideal."

No wonder if those to whom Willie Redmond had been the jester of the House, the " Peter Pan of the Irish party," were amazed at this new avatar ! The Joculator Domini, the Lord's merry-man, when the red day dawned, threw off his motley and went before the knights to the battle. When at this time he was invited to a critical debate in the House, or to some political meeting, he always replied that he could not, even for one day, leave his serious business of training as a soldier. When later on he did make a public appearance, his older looks and more serious demeanour were very noticeable. T. P. O'Connor, for instance, gives us this glimpse of him :

" One day we were told on the quiet that the Irish Brigade was going to have a field-day, with the King and Queen present. . . . I

INTRODUCTION

remember of all that day one incident in particular. . . . The battalions were marching past, and suddenly I saw Willie Redmond marching in front of his own. When I looked at the grizzled hair of this middle-aged man, but a few months before a quiet politician, marching with a blithe step and a look of determination in his set face, I realised what was the heroic spirit behind the man I had known without fathoming for so many years.

"For the first time I saw in his face that curious transformation which had come with the war. Though he was cheerful and equable, the boyishness, the light-hearted spirit, had gone. He was almost unnaturally serious, and often I thought I saw in his expression something of that presentiment which tells the soldier he is going to fall. The grizzled hair, the somewhat thinned face, the alert form, made him an ideal soldier-figure. . . .

"Every time afterward that I saw Willie Redmond the impression he made on me was exactly the same. Here was a man who felt he would die, who nevertheless never swerved for a moment from the determination to face death. On the few occasions when he made his appearance in the House, every one felt towards him that curious mixed sensation

INTRODUCTION

of wonder and sympathy. . . . That quietly set, rather saddened face . . . revealed the man possessed by an ideal; and all the forces of the world might beat for ever in vain against a resolve so great and stern."

Others who knew him are agreed that Willie Redmond foresaw his death. More than that: he may be said to have sought it. He refused to be content with any sort of post, however honourable, which kept him behind the firing-line. Not only was he determined to share danger with his men, not only did his religion lift him above all fear of the end, but he was convinced that his blood would prove a sacrament of unity to his own countrymen, and lift up their hearts to a higher plane.

He went to the front in the winter of 1915; was promoted to Major's rank, and mentioned in despatches by Sir Douglas Haig. At this time he began the series of articles here republished, which were contributed anonymously to the *Daily Chronicle*. Two vivid pictures of Major Redmond in France have been painted for us by Stephen Gwynn:

"In France, regimental officers see little of one another outside their own battalions, and I have only two clear recollections of him in six months. One is our first meeting abroad.

INTRODUCTION

The Rangers were coming out from a very hot time in front of the Hohenzollern Redoubt, and the Royal Irish, as usual, were replacing us. Marching up along the paved road to Bethune, we met them. He was on foot, for he never would ride during a march, and at sight of me he came along the flank of his company with both hands outstretched and his face shining. Such a visage of welcome is not often met, and it even struck the men. 'Dear oh, but the Captain seemed glad to see you!' said one of my sergeants as he passed on. That was his gift—the power of radiating sympathy and affection.

"The second occasion was not a chance meeting. News of the Easter Week rising reached us just as the Brigade was going into the trenches. . . . It seemed to me that after what had happened Irish members were wanted at home, and I went to consult Redmond. His company was in front line, and I found him in the deep head-quarters dugout. He was sitting with the usual papers in front of him—returns to be rendered, reports to be sent in. We went on deck to talk, for it was a fine night in May. 'Anyhow,' I said, 'you are not fit to go on with this.' 'No,' he said, 'I know I am not fit.' Then I upbraided him, because

INTRODUCTION

he had been put to other work out of the trenches, and had given it up. But that, he said, was only a subaltern's job, and a half-time one. He agreed with me, however, about going home, and we parted on the understanding that both should apply for leave. But he never did so. He could not bring himself to leave his post with his company till he actually broke down in health, which happened soon after. When he went back to France, a post was given him on the Divisional Staff."

On March 16, 1916, he appeared in the House to speak on Army Estimates. " One effect of the war on Major Redmond," says the parliamentary correspondent of the *Daily Chronicle*, "was to make him an orator. . . . Willie's interruptions were witty and apposite, but his set speeches seldom hit the mark. The war, stirring him to the depths of his being, unsealed the fount of his eloquence."

A most moving speech, this, in its matter, appealing—how strange there should be need for it !—for a consideration of the war from a human, not an official standpoint. In its manner, it has the direct simplicity of his articles from the trenches. A taste of its quality is to be found in such words as these:

INTRODUCTION

" I am happy to say that I am going back to the front almost immediately. . . . Nothing in the world can depress the spirits of the men that I have seen at the front. I do not believe there were ever enough Germans born into the world to depress them. If it were possible to depress them at all, it can only be done by pursuing a course of embittered controversy in this country as to the right way and wrong way of conducting affairs at the front. . . . All I ask is, that there shall be a truce to carping and criticism, and that when we get a copy of a newspaper out there—and it's not very regularly we get them—that may be an advantage or a disadvantage ; it all depends on the newspaper—we shall not be obliged to read ungenerous and bitter attacks on the public men of all parties, who, I suppose, all present will believe are trying to do their best. . . . If things go pretty well, and the men are comfortable, they say ' Cheer oh ! ' If things go badly, and the snow falls, and the rain comes through the roof of a billet in an impossible sort of cowhouse, they say ' Cheer oh ! ' still more. All we want out there is that you should adopt the same tone, and say ' Cheer oh ! ' to us."

In December (*i.e.* 1916) he spoke again, des-

INTRODUCTION

cribing how Orange and Green fought together in brotherhood on the Somme, and urging them to meet on the floor of the proposed Irish Convention. Charles Lamb, that lover of all mankind, declared that he could never hate any one whom he had actually seen. Whether such a sentiment is common in Ireland, it is not for an English pen to conjecture; that its spirit was in one Irishman is obvious from the whole tone of the speech. It was echoed by Father Donelly in Westminster Cathedral: " Would to God that the whole of Ireland were in Flanders to-day! Then there would be peace."

" These men," said Major Redmond, " who in times of political heat may have been unreasonable in their antagonism, and even in their physical opposition to one another, have recognised in the face of the enemy that they are brother Irishmen. . . . All you want is to get them together. They came together in the trenches, and they were friends; get them together on the floor of an Assembly, or where you will, in Ireland, and it is the opinion of all of us that a similar result will occur. . . . Let them—that is, the Ulstermen—agree to give up their historical memories of events like the Boyne and all the rest. While we will

INTRODUCTION

never forget those who have suffered for our country, we will also give up any celebration that might be irritating, and we will begin and build up out of this war a new and better country, with Protestants and Catholics working side by side—a country based on the recognition of Irishmen."

Are words like these to go down the wind in vain ?

Major Redmond's last appearance before Parliament was on March 7, 1917, when he seconded T. P. O'Connor's motion for immediate Home Rule. It is impossible to read his speech without being moved ; what, then, must have been its effect as delivered by him whom the House " dearly loved," the war-worn figure, speaking without notes, absorbed utterly in his theme ? " Men," says one eyewitness, " listened to the orator spell-bound." " You could hear," relates T. P. O'Connor, " the heavy breathing of men around you, and I was told by one who was in the gallery that men around him sobbed and wept unabashed." This memorable utterance—his dying speech, as it may be called, and profession of faith—is given verbatim in the Appendix.

The end was at hand. When the Great Push came on, in June 1917, he was in per-

INTRODUCTION

manent quarters in the little village of Lœcre, near the parish church, and close to a convent where a field hospital was established—where also the nuns provided baths and good food for the forces. Patrick Sarsfield fell not far off, exclaiming with his last breath, " Would that this blood had been shed for Ireland ! " Here Willie Redmond entertained, not only the Irish Army chaplains, but officers of the Ulster Division. For the account of these last days we cannot do better than quote the words of Father Edmond Kelly, Chaplain to the Forces, in a letter to Monsignor Ryan :

" During the three nights previous to the battle, he and I slept in the cellar under the chapel at the Hospice, and I can assure you that he felt absolutely miserable at the idea of being left behind. He had used every influence with the General to get over the top with the men, and he had little hope of succeeding. He spoke in the most feeling manner of what awaited the poor fellows, and longed to share their suffering and their fate. However, he was not to be denied, and to his extreme delight was given leave to charge with his old battalion of the Royal Irish Regiment. He put on his equipment in Father O'Connell's room, and was simply bubbling over with joy. While

INTRODUCTION

fastening the belts over his shoulders, he was laughing with good humour. 'Won't it be glorious to breast the sand-bags with old George Robey '—a private nickname he had for a great friend of his—' and all the boys ? ' He went up to the trenches accompanied by his servant Organ. When the men saw him, they sent up a cheer. ' Sir,' said Organ, ' this cheering is not good for you ! ' ' I'm afraid, Organ,' answered the Major, ' that you have got shell-shock already.'

" At ten minutes past three on the morning of the 7th, the mines went up, and before the burning earth had time to fall, Major William Redmond, M.P. and founder of the Irish Division, was over the top—the first man in the division to face what to us looked something like an overflow of hell itself. You can form no true idea of the diabolic beauty and fury of the whole scene—the flashes and thunder of a thousand guns, the smell of poisonous gas, the morning light stifled at its birth by the smoke of battle, the cheering of our front battalions. The poor Major fell wounded in the leg and wrist, and, strangely enough, he was found lying on the field by the stretcher-bearers of the Ulster Division. They brought him to their Aid Post, and thence to the Field Ambu-

INTRODUCTION

lance, and there he died. He received every possible kindness from these Ulster soldiers. In fact, an Englishman attached to the Ulster Division expressed some surprise at the extreme care which was taken of the poor Major, though no Irish soldier expected anything else, for after all, the Ulster men are Irish too.

"His body was laid out in the convent chapel, before the altar where you used to say Mass last Christmas, and he was buried quietly on the evening of June 8, near the grotto in the nuns' garden. May God have mercy on his soul! No purer-hearted man, no braver soldier, ever died on the battlefield. He was absolutely convinced that he was dying for Ireland. . . . In my humble opinion, Willie Redmond deserves the admiration of every man capable of admiring sanctity in a Catholic, valour in a soldier, and the most unselfish love of country in a patriot."

The wisdom of those dark ages which, around hearth-fire or hunter's fire, by ice-grey sea or in illimitable forests, embodied itself in the folk-lore of Northern Europe, has told us by a thousand stories of shape-changing or transformation that human blood poured out is the sure magical means of delivering the human captive doomed to wear the beast's

INTRODUCTION

likeness. This truth, then, before the advent even of Christianity, was bred in the very bones of our race. Here, in this book, we see how the Dark Rosaleen found a lover who poured out his life to win healing for her soul. Sigurd the Dragon-slayer—King Arthur—Joan of Arc—the procession of heroes emerges from darkness, passing from hand to hand the flaming sword of the Spirit. The generations come and go; in no generation is the torch-bearer lacking. The heart of our own generation, purged by pity and terror, recognises that, last in the order of time, but not least in the order of heroic succession, it has seen such a torch-bearer in the person of Willie Redmond.

I
A GARDEN TRENCH

I

A GARDEN TRENCH

(August 17, 1916)

THERE is a certain trench on the Western front well known and much traversed by our troops. It is one of the oldest trenches, and was once in the possession of the enemy in the days when the enemy held that particular part of France.

Trenches are much alike, and there is as a rule nothing in the world to distinguish one from the other, save here and there at junctions and corners, boards which bear names just as names appear at street corners. And it is the practice to give the trenches the

TRENCH PICTURES

names of well-known streets at home. There are English, Scotch, Irish, and Welsh names; and most of the best known London street-names figure in the list.

When a subaltern is told on a wet and miserable night to take out a working party, and when he is informed that his destination is "Shaftesbury Avenue," or Piccadilly, or Regent Street, it does not improve his temper. He trudges off, feeling keenly no doubt the strong contrast between his muddy surroundings in the trench, and the London thoroughfare which calls before his mind prospects, very likely dim and distant, of leave which may or may not come.

The trench of which I am thinking and writing had no alluring London name, but it is nevertheless well known, and its name, which need not be mentioned, is quite familiar to thousands of troops. A long and weary trench it is,

A GARDEN TRENCH

representing long and weary labour. Many of the men who dug it are now at rest for ever, but their work remains and will remain till the arrival of that day when labour shall be employed in filling and not in digging trenches. And what a task that will be! And how long a time will have to pass before the war-stricken fields of France and Belgium recover from the frightful mangling which shot and shell and tramping feet have caused!

In winter time the trench in my mind's eye is dark, damp, forbidding, and gloomy. A veritable lane of agony, where weary feet fall and where no single bright spot redeems the dullness or catches the eye. That is in winter.

In summer the trench is transformed. Along the top at each side there are real flower-beds, running almost the full length of the way. Not indeed flower-beds planted by the hands of gardeners, but flower-beds far more beautiful than ever planted by human hands—flower-beds which are the handiwork of Nature unaided.

Poppies red and cornflowers blue spread along in marvellous profusion. Daisies white and yellow, and long sprays of graceful grass, with here and there scraps of waving corn, the wild product of some long-ago sowing, before the land was ploughed with shot and shell. The ears of corn blend with the red poppies in far more graceful arrangement than ever was designed by even the most skilful florist hand.

It is a bare, level plain where this garden trench, as I call it, stretches; and the wind sweeping along has carried the wild flower seeds far and wide, and they have rooted in the loosely turned soil along the trench top. A more wonderful contrast it would be hard to imagine than that afforded by the wonderful

A GARDEN TRENCH

profusion of wild flowers peering down and the dark depths below.

On the Western front, at certain parts, the land where two great armies contend is more or less on a dead level. Viewed from above the whole country seems one bare bleak plain. No trees, no hedges, no fences—nothing save here and there the wire entanglements before some redoubt or specially guarded trench. And, most remarkable of all, there is no sign of human life. Yet beneath the surface of the earth are thousands and thousands of men, on the alert, and leading an ordered and disciplined existence.

In winter time this stretch of bleak country, for the possession of which two great armies contend, is forbidding in all its aspects—a waste of trampled mud. In summer it is ablaze with wild flowers. The hum of bee and the song of bird are in the air, and but for the

TRENCH PICTURES

thick unhealthy clouds of smoke which follow the bursting shells that drop ever and anon with a mighty crash, the spectator might imagine he was contemplating some scene of wild land untrodden by man. There is nothing more striking than the difference between the fighting area of the West in summer and in winter, and this change has its effect upon the combatants.

The mass of wild flowers everywhere is remarkable. As the soldiers pass their weary way to and fro along the trenches, the blossoms along each side wave and nod as though encouraging them. And the wounded, as they are carried along on the stretchers through the trench, pass, one might say, along an avenue of flowers, and have their minds carried back to the fields and pleasant places of their native land.

Now and again a gust of wind will blow the petals of the flaming poppies

A GARDEN TRENCH

down, and they lie at the bottom, looking against the brown clay like bright red drops of blood. Whilst human beings day and night slaughter each other, Nature marches her course unruffled. The flowers bloom, the birds sing through the very smoke of battle, and even the trenches, the very paths to destruction, are lavishly decorated by Nature's hand and made beautiful, as though in mockery of the waste and horror created by war-waging man.

And here and there, amidst the tangle of wild flowers on the plains that have been fought over, have been planted thousands of the little rude wooden crosses which roughly mark the last resting-places of the fallen. In winter these little memorials seem grim and lonely. Not so under the summer sun, for then they are garlanded and bedecked by Nature with a lavish hand.

The writer came the other day upon

TRENCH PICTURES

the roughly made cross of wood which marked the grave of a French infantryman. His name and regiment were rudely carved on the cross, with the date of his death, and beneath were the words, in French, "Dead on the Field of Honour."

Those who were dear to this soldier may never have an opportunity of standing by his grave or tending it. They need not grieve, however, for Nature has done all that could be required or wished for. A quilt of wildflowers covers this humble resting-place, and red poppies and blue cornflowers nestle around the little cross, and with every breath of wind nod and point to the words, "Dead on the Field of Honour!"

So it is. Whilst man makes the earth hideous and lacerates it with shot and shell, Nature gently covers up the ravages of war and makes even the

A GARDEN TRENCH

grave and the trench very often beautiful. All of which but goes to prove, as one of our chaplains said, that there is after all a Power higher and mightier than the power of the " All Highest War Lord.".

II

TO CHARING CROSS VIA THE RED CROSS

II

TO CHARING CROSS VIA THE RED CROSS

(September 11, 1916)

WHATEVER criticisms or complaints may be heard from time to time as to other departments connected with the war, it is true to say that there is general agreement as to the very excellent way in which the R.A.M.C. have conducted their most urgent and important work.

As a matter of fact, there is very little complaining at all on the part of the soldier abroad — certainly in France. Hardships and trials of all kinds are encountered and borne with splendid forti-

TRENCH PICTURES

tude. This fine spirit is very largely the result of the comforting feeling which the soldier has, that should wounds or sickness be his lot he is able to count on the very best of care. Directly a man in the field is stricken down, he receives the most prompt and skilful and careful treatment.

How many of the crowds who in sympathy assemble at Charing Cross and other stations to watch the arrival of the wounded from the front, realise the speed and skill with which the wounded men have been conveyed home?

The organisation of the Army Medical Corps, aided by the Red Cross and the many other kindred associations, is simply a marvel of devoted labour and scientific arrangement. In many cases little more than twenty-four hours elapse from the time a man is wounded in the front line to the time when he finds himself, cleansed and comfortable

TO CHARING CROSS VIA RED CROSS

and safe, in the bed of some London hospital.

Let those who contribute to Red Cross work, and particularly to motor ambulance funds, feel quite sure that they get full value for their money in the help and comfort they have brought to those who need help and comfort most—the men who have shed their blood at the front in defence of the Line.

The writer has seen the work of the R.A.M.C. right from the trench to the hospital. It is a very wonderful chain which links the trench with London, and every link is as nearly perfect as possible. Begin at the trench. A man is wounded on the fire step. With little delay his wound is treated with first-aid appliances, either by his nearest comrade or by the stretcher-bearers—devoted men who are ever at their posts and ready under all circumstances. The little "first-aid" packet which every soldier carries is taken from the wounded soldier's pocket. His clothes are cut to expose the wound, which is at once roughly dressed.

If the man can walk he is brought to the trench dressing station, or if he cannot walk he is carried on a stretcher. At the dressing station the battalion doctor treats the wound, and the man is taken down from the trenches to the nearest field ambulance, where his wound is again dealt with.

If the soldier can be moved with safety a Red Cross motor hurries him to the nearest field hospital. If the wound is of a sufficiently serious nature to claim prolonged treatment, he is, as soon as possible, placed in an ambulance train with comfortable fittings and skilled nurses. The train is timed to meet the ambulance ship at the port of embarkation, and the wounded man is carefully carried on board, and in due

TO CHARING CROSS VIA RED CROSS

course arrives at Charing Cross or whatever the station may be, and so on to one of the many hospitals now available.

In many cases, as I say, the transfer from the grimy trench and the sound of the guns, to the comfort and peace of the home hospital, is all carried out in very little more than the twenty-four hours of the day and the night.

So it is that thousands of men are conveyed home every week. It all represents a most wonderful and efficient and never-resting organisation of devoted men and women, commencing with the stretcher-bearers on the field, and ending only with the doctors and nurses in the home hospital.

Probably in the world's history no such perfect arrangements have ever been made for the care of the wounded and the sick. This, of course, refers particularly to the wounded from France and Belgium.

TRENCH PICTURES

Happy, indeed, would be the stricken on the more distant fronts could they be conveyed home with the same celerity. To the members of the R.A.M.C. of all ranks in this war, too much praise cannot be given. From the most highly placed doctors to the youngest stretcher-bearers, they deserve the warmest thanks of the Army and the country. Be it remembered also that these men do their duty at the very front in large numbers, and that many of the field ambulances are under constant fire.

The work of the R.A.M.C. is performed under circumstances of difficulty and danger little dreamt of by many people at home. The rudest kind of shelter in the trench, or amidst ruined walls, is often all the protection the surgeon and his assistants have, and very often indeed they have to tend the wounded on the open field itself.

Every one of the wounded men we see

TO CHARING CROSS VIA RED CROSS

arriving at Charing Cross has reached home via the Red Cross service; that is to say, from the moment he leaves the trench till he arrives in London, he has passed through the hands of a devoted and heroic band of men and women—doctors, nurses, and attendants—who have ceaselessly tended him on stretcher, on hospital bed, on motorcar, on train, and on barge and boat.

The cases which cannot at once be dealt with by transfer to the home hospitals are treated in the stationary hospitals somewhat back from the line; and these establishments have been instituted and equipped with a thoroughness and up-to-date scientific arrangement which would do credit to any hospitals in the whole world.

The writer recently visited two of these places in the north of France, one having for its headquarters an old château, and the other a large school.

TRENCH PICTURES

Nothing could have been better than these hospitals, nowhere could the comfort of the wounded be more closely studied, and nowhere could more skilful surgery or more trained and careful nursing be found.

To visit one of these establishments, as Mr. Asquith did not so long ago, one might have thought that they were the result of years of thought and labour on the spot. But, on the contrary, the hospitals have just sprung into existence with the necessities of the war.

Everything, literally everything, had to be done, to fashion and shape unlikely places into suitable hospital accommodation. Swiftly and well has the work been done under the skill and energy of the R.A.M.C. Everything is as perfect as work and tireless energy and skill can achieve. Wards spotlessly clean, filled with rows and rows of beds also spotlessly clean; operating rooms, with the latest appliances of science; baths and stores, kitchens and playgrounds, even; and gardens filled with flowers, where the convalescent may take the air, and gradually draw back the strength of which cruel wounds have robbed them.

These mushroom hospitals behind the fighting line are indeed a continual source of wonder to those who see them, and who take the trouble to reflect on all that has had to be done quickly, and in the face of all sorts of difficulties.

And all the time the movement and change in these havens of mercy and rest go on. Hundreds of new patients arrive, and hundreds leave by boat or barge or train or car constantly, either for the coast or back to the line. And as each particular patient comes, he is dealt with separately and carefully. His clothes are taken and cleansed and labelled till he needs them. His rifle and his equipment are similarly dealt with;

TRENCH PICTURES

and when he is ready for transfer or discharge, his belongings are ready to his hand, bright, clean, and complete in every way.

Nothing that is needed for the recovery and comfort of the wounded soldier is overlooked, and—it will interest the taxpayer to learn—economy is practised where possible and consistent with efficiency. All improvements and light labour about these places are done as far as possible by convalescents who are able for work, and who indeed are glad to be of use to those of their comrades who are not so far recovered as themselves.

The colonel of the R.A.M.C. at the head of one of these splendid hospitals, who was so good as to spare a little time in showing me round, noticed that I very much admired the really beautiful flowers in the grounds. "Oh!" said he, "don't think we employ gardeners. Those flower beds were made by one of

TO CHARING CROSS VIA RED CROSS

the convalescents. There he is. He was a gardener to the Duke of —— before he joined the New Army."

And so, according to their trades, the convalescent men help the hospitals and do something to make them better for those who may come after them. The napkin rings and salt cellars on the officers' mess table were fashioned by a soldier tinsmith out of old biscuit boxes !

As in the trenches, so also in these hospitals; when he is able, Tommy does his little bit to help things along. Long rows of tents stretching away on either side of the château I found to be equipped with beds, in the warm weather of summer forming the coolest and most comfortable hospital wards imaginable.

Every conceivable ailment I found provided for. For the teeth a dental department with everything necessary, and a large staff and specialists. The same

TRENCH PICTURES

provision and care for the eye—eye specialists, with their assistants, testing the eyes of the men and supplying suitable glasses where required. Everything is thought of, everything is done for the men, and it has all come about so suddenly that the completeness of the arrangements is marvellous.

To speak personally, the writer of these lines visited this particular hospital for a little eye trouble of his own. He had the attention and examination, as any Tommy might, of an eye specialist from Harley Street. And this within an hour or so of the front line. It just illustrates the way in which things are done and the way in which the medical men of the country have come to do their bit, leaving home and comfort, ay, and good practices, too, behind them.

From the school which I have mentioned as one of the hospitals visited, all the pupils had gone, but the

TO CHARING CROSS VIA RED CROSS

members of the Order of Teaching Brothers had remained. Venerable old Frenchmen, they glided with noiseless steps here and there about the corridors, and smiled as they passed the doctors and nurses, seeming quite glad that their monastery should be used for so beautiful a purpose as sheltering the stricken in war.

In one of the wards I noticed all the suffering had head injuries, and some of them did indeed seem dreadfully wounded. It made one's heart feel heavy—the sight of so many men in the springtime of youth suffering so much. Yet coming away one felt glad at heart also to see the care taken of our wounded: the wards were so beautifully kept, with flowers here and there, and the glare of the August sunshine was carefully shaded from the pale faces in the beds.

Who can estimate how much has

TRENCH PICTURES

been done by the women who have crossed the seas and come to nurse the soldiers? Who can ever properly repay them? One can only say now and always, " Hats off to the brave nurses in this war, and God bless them!" That is, at any rate, how the writer of these lines felt after visiting these hospitals—situated, be it remembered, within an easy drive of the firing trenches.

As we left the building a number of newly arrived wounded men were being received in the corridor. There they lay, with eyes closed, very quietly, on the stretchers. One felt glad to know, and every helper of the Red Cross should feel glad to know, that these poor victims of the war will, at any rate, receive all the aid that skill and devoted care can give them in these hospitals, which are an everlasting tribute to the R.A.M.C.

As we drove away back towards the

TO CHARING CROSS VIA RED CROSS

front the bell in the old school chapel began gently to clang out the *Angelus*, calling the aged monks to prayer, and it was a very pleasant sound, and soothing and appropriate too.

III
AS THEY FOUGHT, SO THEY DIED

III

AS THEY FOUGHT, SO THEY DIED

(September 13, 1916)

It is in a cemetery in France, one of those cemeteries which have sprung up during the war, and where the graves are all quite new. All around, the little crosses bear the names of men belonging to many British regiments; with here and there French names, under which are inscribed the words "Mort pour La France."

Two graves lie open, waiting to receive the dead; close by, a group of officers stand, and the men who have made the graves are in the background leaning on their spades. A little way off, an old man and some women are busy saving a field of corn, and the whirring noise of a reaping machine sounds drowsily on the air.

From a greater distance comes the dull roar of guns, and overhead an aeroplane circles like some giant bird. The group of officers by the grave side includes two chaplains, one Church of England and one a Catholic priest. They have come to bury two young officers, both Irish, but of different Churches.

Presently a little procession arrives: a motor wagon, looking strangely incongruous in the cemetery, and behind it a little company of the men belonging to the regiment of the dead officers. They stand around the opened earth like statues, their faces set in an expression of pain. The eyes of some are filled with tears, for they knew well and loved their young leaders—young, indeed, they were: merely boys.

AS THEY FOUGHT, SO THEY DIED

Reverently the remains are lifted to the grave; there are no coffins here. The bodies, swathed in the ordinary brown Army blankets, are lowered into the grave side by side, shoulder to shoulder, just as in life the boys had lain in their rude shelter in the trenches for many days and many nights. The chaplains read the burial services of their respective Churches. "Ashes to ashes dust to dust." Some soil of France is shovelled into the graves, and soon the little group of mourners melts away.

As the men of the dead officers' regiment march off, they gaze up reverently as they pass by the great Crucifix in the centre of the cemetery. It is to them not only a symbol of the hope of salvation, but a symbol of the glory and majesty of a death suffered for the sake of others. And so the soldiers pass along, more reconciled to the loss of their two young leaders, for they cer-

TRENCH PICTURES

tainly did suffer death bravely and most willingly for the sake of others—for the sake of those at home in the country they loved.

One of these gallant young officers was twenty-two, the other but twenty-one. They left Ireland with hearts overflowing with the joy of life, and with that glorious spirit of youth which fills the world with a seemingly never-fading beauty and happiness. One boy left his University, and the other the threshold of a great profession, and they went to the trenches of France, where they met death absolutely without fear.

And every month thousands of all ranks are dying thus. In the cemetery where the writer stood by the graves of these two boys he counted in one tiny corner alone, eleven white crosses newly erected. Each of these crosses bore the name of a young Irish officer, and in

AS THEY FOUGHT, SO THEY DIED

only one instance was the recorded age more than twenty-five years.

These young men came from the North of Ireland and from the South, with the famous Irish regiments—the Connaught Rangers, the Dublin Fusiliers, the Irish Rifles, the Munsters, the Leinsters, the Inniskillings, or the Royal Irish. They professed different creeds; they held different views on politics and public affairs; but they were knitted and welded into one by a common cause. They fought side by side for their country, they died side by side, and in this little French cemetery, with the great cross, they lie side by side in their last long sleep.

And so to-day do Irishmen rest in all the fields in the long-stretched battle lines of Europe. Would that all those who still may harbour bitterness and rancour against any of their own countrymen in Ireland might stand for even one moment and read the cross inscriptions

TRENCH PICTURES

in the cemeteries of France! Those inscriptions which tell of the glorious and eternal union of brave Protestant and Catholic, and Northern and Southern Irish hearts!

IV

THE TAKING OF GINCHY

IV

THE TAKING OF GINCHY

(*September* 19, 1916)

Irish Regiments which took part in the capture of Guillemont behaved with the greatest dash and gallantry, and took no small share in the success gained that day.—Sir Douglas Haig's report, September 8.

The fine work of Irish troops from Connaught, Leinster, and Munster, already mentioned in connection with the capture of Guillemont, was carried on yesterday by the same troops in the attack on Ginchy.—Sir Douglas Haig's report, September 10.

TRENCH PICTURES

THE Germans surrendered very freely, and in very few instances waited for the bayonets of the Irish. When able, the enemy made good his retreat, but when this was not possible he surrendered and threw down his arms. In some cases, however, treachery was attempted.

I met a Munster Fusilier who in the confusion of the battle had got separated from his battalion. He was resting by the road waiting to find some one who could direct him to his headquarters. He was covered with mud, but full of genuine enthusiasm.

I asked if his battalion had made many prisoners. He replied "Yes"; but added that once or twice the Germans had tried treacherous tricks. One party advanced as if to surrender, shouting "Kamerad! Kamerad!" and when about twenty yards

THE TAKING OF GINCHY

off opened fire. I asked the Munster man what then took place, and he replied, "We knocked them over till further orders."

In almost every case, however, the Germans came in freely and willingly. There could be no mistaking their relief when their surrender was accepted, or their delighted surprise at being treated decently. They presented—even the officers—a woebegone appearance; and it transpired that for three days it had been impossible to supply them with rations or water, so terrific had been the British artillery fire.

All the prisoners asked at once, some in English and others by gesture, for water, which was of course supplied to them. Those who were wounded were most kindly looked after by the surgeons, and also by the chaplains of all denominations.

TRENCH PICTURES

An Irish Catholic priest was very eagerly surrounded by some of the prisoners—Bavarians—and they were more than pleased when wounded to receive the chaplain's ministrations. Some of the Germans spōke a little English, and the chaplain had some slight knowledge of German, so that conversation was possible.

One prisoner said: "We do not want war—it is the war of the rich man, and the poor always suffer."

Another man, who was wounded, begged the chaplain to write to his mother in Germany to let her know he was safe. The prisoners were utilised to carry the stretchers with our wounded, and they seemed quite willing to help in this work.

Nearly all the Irish possessed some trophies of the fight, and it was a common sight to see even the wounded on the stretchers clutching in their hands Ger-

THE TAKING OF GINCHY

man helmets, electric torches, and bits of enemy equipment.

At the advanced dressing station the scene was wonderful. Prisoners and our wounded came in in streams, and it was terrible to see the suffering of the men. But suffering was borne most bravely, and the uppermost sentiment seemed to be one of intense pride that the Irish regiments had done the work allotted to them.

Many of our wounded were just boys, and it was extraordinary how they bore pain which must have been intense. Very few murmurings were heard. One young man said to the chaplain, "Oh, Father, it is hard to die so far from home in the wilds of France!" Certainly the fair land of France just here did seem wild — the trees all torn and riven with shot and the earth on every side ploughed with huge shell holes.

TRENCH PICTURES

The prisoners seemed very anxious to know where they were to be sent, and one or two asked if there were any chance of their being sent to England, where they were very anxious to go. It is hard to judge men who are prisoners and dishevelled and without equipment, but it was very noticeable that the Germans were by no means as smart as our own men. The grey uniform is not attractive, and in most cases it appeared ill-fitting and gave an awkward appearance to the prisoners.

Physically, these prisoners were mostly imposing, but here and there very miserable specimens of humanity were observed, and naturally they all wore a very dejected expression. Whenever an officer passed they sprang to attention with an almost startled look, as though they were afraid.

The Irishmen, while clearly immensely pleased with themselves, showed no

THE TAKING OF GINCHY

undue exultation, and their demeanour towards their captives was good-humoured and even kind. It was pleasant to see how tenderly they helped the wounded Germans along; and down the road from the dressing station, it was a common sight to see our men helping along prisoners just as kindly as if they were their own comrades.

The losses in the Irish battalions were naturally heavy, but by no means very great in view of the work that had been done. Some very valuable officers fell, notably Colonel Lennox Cuningham, who was killed leading his battalion very gallantly in the attack. He was buried close by in a little churchyard behind the lines, amidst every possible manifestation of grief and respect.

Other gallant officers fell similarly, including Major Naylor, of the Royal Irish Regiment.

TRENCH PICTURES

Alike before, during, and after the attack on Guillemont the British guns were incessantly in action. The artillery is wonderful, and the common comment on it all is one of high compliment to the munition workers at home, without whose labour the men at the front would be indeed powerless. In this battle of Guillemont it should be borne in mind that the Irish regiments were opposed by picked German troops—Brandenburgers.

A few days after the attack on Guillemont, the whole Irish Division, comprising battalions of all the famous Irish regiments, entered the line and joined in an advance which was attended with success, but also with considerable losses. The Irish troops have certainly borne a fair share in the fighting on the Somme. First the Ulster Division, and subsequently another division brilliantly capturing Guillemont; and then, within

THE TAKING OF GINCHY

four or five days, Ginchy—a specially fine achievement.

At 3.45 on September 9 the latter division advanced upon Ginchy. The regiments comprising it had had a hard and trying time for many months in the trenches farther north, and had had little or no rest. Nevertheless, the men went to work with positive enthusiasm, and, in spite of a terrible barrage by enemy artillery and rifle and machine-gun fire, they carried all before them.

Three of the Irish regiments—from Leinster, Connaught, and Munster—had only a few days before won Guillemont; but, nevertheless, even these battalions advanced with much spirit and dash.

Several previous efforts had been made to capture Ginchy, but it was "reserved" for this division to accomplish that very important achieve-

TRENCH PICTURES

ment. The losses were high, for the work was of a very difficult nature, but the result of capturing Ginchy will have far-reaching effects upon the whole campaign; and this is not the only or the main compensation for losses sustained.

It is not too much to say that the whole Army on the Somme has expressed warm admiration for the action of the Irish troops; and the capture of Ginchy, coming hot-foot on the taking of Guillemont, has put, it is safe to say, an entirely new complexion on the whole position in this part of the line on the Somme.

A captured German officer declared that his people had believed that Ginchy could not be taken. "But," he added, "you attacked us with devils, not men — no one could withstand them."

A notable feature of the charge on

THE TAKING OF GINCHY

Ginchy was that the Irishmen sang Irish patriotic songs, one battalion to the other, as they charged, and the effect created was most inspiring.

V

THE CAMP-FIRE PRAYER

V

THE CAMP-FIRE PRAYER

(September 26, 1916)

THE men were encamped, or, rather, bivouacked, on the bare side of a hill. They had no cover, no tents, and simply lay upon the ground with such small shelter as their waterproof sheets afforded them.

It was a bleak and desolate scene, relieved only here and there by the bright sparkle of little fires around which the Irish soldiers clustered.

Bleak and desolate as the prospect was, the spirits of the men were high and buoyant. Some of them sang, others were busy in cleaning their rifles

TRENCH PICTURES

and equipment. Bursts of laughter rang out in the darkness.

It was really wonderful, passing through the many groups, to notice the entire absence of anything like depression. Yet these men who lay about upon the bare earth had but newly arrived after a long and weary march over a bad road, and during a perfectly terrible downpour of rain.

Everybody knew that the next day was to be the day of battle—the day for which for nearly two years the new battalions had trained, ever since they first came together on the banks of the Blackwater away in Ireland.

It really and truly seemed as if it were the very prospect of the struggle on the morrow which kept these damp and travel-stained fellows in good heart!

Yet each man knew, deep in his heart, that, by the next night, many of them would have gone for ever.

THE CAMP-FIRE PRAYER

At one side of the hill where the men lay, a fife-and-drum band was playing well-known Irish airs, and they were listened to with keen appreciation and rewarded by cheers.

There was no uncertainty in the minds of the men as to the result of the attack which they were about to make. "It's all right; we shall have Guillemont tomorrow." That is what they said, and they said it with a conviction which was impressive, and yet without boasting or arrogance.

At the same time, these men, so gay and light-hearted, are filled with the deepest and purest feelings of religion. The majority of these Irish soldiers are Roman Catholics, and even those who cannot agree with the doctrines of that creed, never fail to admire the devotion and steadfastness with which the Irishmen adhere to their faith under all circumstances.

TRENCH PICTURES

On the particular night to which the writer refers, just as the camp-fires were dying down and the men were preparing to wrap themselves in their coats for the rest which they might be able to snatch, an officer came over the side of the hill and down to the centre of the camp.

It was the Catholic chaplain—a devoted priest who had been with the Irish troops in Ireland, in England, and in France, and whose never-ceasing work is keenly appreciated by all ranks. In a moment he was surrounded by the men. They came to him without orders—they came gladly and willingly—and they hailed his visit with manifest delight. He spoke to them in the simple, homely language which they liked.

He spoke of the sacrifice which they had made, in freely and promptly leaving their homes to fight for a cause which was the cause of religion, freedom and civilisation.

THE CAMP-FIRE PRAYER

He reminded them that in this struggle they were most certainly defending the homes and the relations and friends they had left behind them in Ireland. It was a simple, yet most moving address, and deeply affected the soldiers.

When the chaplain had finished his address he signed to the men to kneel, and administered to them the General Absolution given in times of emergency. The vast majority of the men present knelt, and those of other faith stood by in attitudes of reverent respect. The chaplain then asked the men to recite with him the Rosary.

It was most wonderful, the effect produced as hundreds and hundreds of voices repeated the prayers and recited the words " Pray for us now and at the hour of our death. Amen."

VI

HOW THE COLONEL CAME BACK

VI

HOW THE COLONEL CAME BACK

(*October* 6, 1916)

THE field kitchens had gone up the long dark road in the direction where the division had been engaged in action. It was a very successful action, and all the news which trickled back was very cheering.

True, there had been many, many losses, both in officers and men, but even these, saddening as they were, were almost forgotten for the time in the exultation felt at what had been achieved.

The division had gone through most gloriously. The position to be assaulted had already, in the course of the long drawn-out battle, been assaulted six times, but without success.

For two years the Germans had been entrenched there, and they had, as well they know how, made the position very strong. Barbed-wire entanglements of the most intricate kind; machine-gun emplacements where the guns, by cunningly contrived lifts, could disappear during bombardment and reappear at once afterwards. Everything that could be contrived to ward off attacks had been contrived, and quite openly the enemy boasted that the place was impregnable.

Now, however, the joyful news came that in the seventh attack the " old Irish Division " had won through.

The following day the victorious battalions worked hard " consolidating " the ground won and digging themselves in to resist counter-attacks. When night came they would be relieved by fresh troops;

HOW THE COLONEL CAME BACK

and so when night did come, and it came loweringly, with angry, black clouds sweeping across the moon, the field kitchens were sent up the long dark road down which the men would march from the battlefield.

Midway along the road some of the battalions would bivouac for the night at each side. So the transport officers hurried off the field kitchens to meet them and to prepare hot soup, tea, and everything possible for the weary soldiers who for two days and two nights had been fighting and advancing with only such food as they might carry in their haversacks.

This long, dark road was intermittently shelled; but had it been shelled on every yard of it the transport men would willingly have gone up it to meet their battle-worn comrades.

The great majority of the wounded had been picked up and dealt with; but after an action, wounded men are encountered singly and in little groups—men who have been sheltering in shell-holes and unable for the time to reach assistance or make their plight known.

From these returning sufferers much information is gleaned by the men of the transport as they pass along. Comrades are inquired for and officers asked after. Sometimes the answer is "Dead," sometimes "Wounded," and sometimes it is hard to get definite news.

On the night to which the writer refers the transport men of a certain battalion asked many questions of the men they met coming down from the front. Nearly all the questions included inquiries as to the colonel. "How is the old C.O.? Is he all right?" Particularly anxiously did the colonel's groom ask this question.

At last there is the steady noise of marching feet. The battalion has arrived, and all is stir about the kitchens.

HOW THE COLONEL CAME BACK

The colonel's servant meets a man of his own company, very tired, very muddy, and very careworn-looking. "Hullo, Pat! Glad to see you, old man! Is the C.O. come?"

Pat stops suddenly, and looks up a little startled and surprised.

"The C.O.? Yes, ah, yes! The C.O. has come!" And heartily rejoiced at the news, the colonel's servant hurries off to the cook sergeant for the hot tea he has arranged to be ready for his master.

Even the most weary and worn-out soldiers let their tongues wag when they come to the field kitchens and know that some hot food is at hand.

It is strange to-night, though, how silent the men are. They sink to the ground slowly, they seem even indifferent to the greetings of the transport men—they even ignore the kitchens!

The colonel's servant comes hurrying

along with a steaming cup in his hand. He stops near the shelter he has put up for his master behind the wagon. There is an officer standing close by. "Very glad to see you safe, captain! Is the colonel here, sir?"

The officer looks up, his face haggard. Pointing to the shelter, he replies to the servant in a low voice, "Yes, oh, yes, the colonel is here." Very eagerly the servant goes towards the rude shelter, saying, "Colonel, indeed I am glad you are back. I have your tea, sir; or perhaps you would like a little soup; or else maybe———"

The officer interrupts him, and, laying his hand upon his shoulder, says: "Don't you understand, man?—the colonel———"

The two men stare at each other. In a flash the servant now understands! Very tenderly they raise the covering from the body, and by the light of an

HOW THE COLONEL CAME BACK

electric torch they look at the calm, dead face.

Yes, the colonel is here. He might, indeed, be sleeping, so peaceful he seems, his hands clasped across his breast, over the mud-stained and blood-stained uniform. A long, cruel gash spreads over one cheek—not disfiguring but rather, indeed, ennobling the more the face which the men had always thought looked noble.

When the morning dawned they carried him, mourning and with respect, to the graveyard in the little ruined town near by.

And thus it was the colonel came back with his battalion.

VII

IN THE DARKENED CHURCH

VII

IN THE DARKENED CHURCH

(January 29, 1917)

IT is true, alas! that in the war zone—that is to say, close by the very front—there is little to be seen that is other than saddening, pitiful, and wounding to the feelings of those who cling to the civilisation of the Christian era. The ruined homes, the wasted fields, the evidences of destruction and rapine upon all sides, may well make men almost despair of humanity.

The "pomp and glory" of modern war are trivial things compared to the devastation of the invaded land and the misery of its wretched inhabitants. Glory there

TRENCH PICTURES

is, indeed, for those who, with their bodies, their hearts and souls, defend the Right; but of glory there is assuredly none attaching to the work of the German hordes who ruthlessly laid waste the poor little land of Belgium, and enslaved a people whose chief characteristics were fear of God and love of industry.

And yet in the very welter of ruin and devastation, and amidst all the havoc wrought by men in their most brutal mood, one comes here and there across little scenes which, at a stroke, seem to restore one's faith in mankind, and one's trust that the Power which, from nothing, made the world beautiful, will yet stay the frenzied work of the man whose god seems to be the dripping sword alone.

At a certain point at the front there is a village where the troops come from time to time to rest, and the church there is crowded each evening with the soldiers.

IN THE DARKENED CHURCH

Lights of a brilliant kind are not allowed in this village as it is so near the line, and it is urgent at night to give no sign which might make the place a target for the long-range guns of the enemy. Therefore the church is never lighted in the evening, and it is by the flames of a few candles alone on the altar of Our Lady of Dolores that the Rosary is recited.

It is a strange scene in this church at night. Entering it, all is dark save for the few flickering candles on the altar before which the priest kneels to say the prayers. It is only when the men join in, that one becomes aware that the church is really full; and it is solemn and appealing—beyond words to describe—when up from the darkness rises the great chorus of hundreds of voices in prayer. The darkness seems to add impressiveness to the prayers, whilst from the outside are heard the rumble and roar of the guns which, not so very

TRENCH PICTURES

far away, are dealing out death and agony to the comrades of the men who are praying. Sometimes the church is momentarily illumined by the flashes of the guns, and the windows are lighted up as though by lightning.

The writer of these lines has seen many an impressive spectacle of large congregations at prayer in great and spacious churches in many lands, but nothing more truly touching, impressive, and moving has he ever witnessed than the darkened church behind the lines, thronged with troops fervently invoking the intercession of the Mother of God under almost the very shadow of the wings of the Angel of Death.

In France and Belgium the Catholic troops are fortunate in having at hand so many churches of their own faith, and this makes it easier for the devoted chaplains to get their flocks together. For so many days the battalions are in the

IN THE DARKENED CHURCH

trenches, and for so many days in the comparative safety of the camps in the little villages somewhere back from the firing line.

The day and night before a battalion goes to the trenches, the chaplains are busy in the churches, for the men throng to confession; and it is a wonderful and most faith-inspiring sight to see them in hundreds approaching the altar before marching off to danger, and in many cases to death itself.

When the turn in the trenches is over, and the men resume their Rosary in the darkened church in the evenings, there are always some absent ones who were there the week before. For this very reason perhaps—because of the comrades who will never kneel by their side again, the men pray all the more fervently, and with ever-increasing earnestness say, " May the souls of the Faithful departed through the mercy of God rest in peace ! "

TRENCH PICTURES

Whilst some of the chaplains attend the men who are resting in the back villages, others follow the men into the line, and there, in some ruined house close by, or in a shelter or dug-out in the trench itself, they are always at hand to minister to the suffering and the dying. Who can measure the consolation they bring, or who can describe the comfort and happiness of the soldier whose eyes, before they close for ever, rest upon the face of the priest of his own faith? If the priest in peace is the ever-sought comforter of the afflicted and dying, how much more so is the priest in time of war and in the battle line!

The writer has met at the front many chaplains, and the dominant feeling of one and all is thankfulness that they were able to go out with the men and share their lot.

Of all the actors in the great tragedy

IN THE DARKENED CHURCH

of the war none stand out more heroically than the chaplains, none fill a greater place in what has come to be called the theatre of war. No wonder so many of them have received decorations, and no wonder the men highly value the presence and the consolation and the encouragement of the "Padre," as the officers call all the ministers of religion.

To the Catholic soldiers, however, the priest remains "Father," and it is good to see them smile as he approaches, and to hear the sound ring of the old faith in their voices as they reply to his salutation and address him always as "Father." Mass has been said in the very trenches, and the writer has attended Mass in many a ruined church and many a shell-wrecked shelter. And ever and always the men are the same—devoted and earnest, and the more wretched their surroundings, the more eager they are.

Nothing is more noticeable than the

TRENCH PICTURES

way the Catholic soldier holds by his beads. In the change and chance and turmoil of active service many things get lost, but the Rosary beads seem to be always treasured, and every soldier at Mass seems to have them. Prayer books are often missing, but the Rosary, as a rule, never is.

The writer has seen men who were killed in the line. Their little personal belongings are carefully collected by comrades and safely kept to be sent home; but the Rosary, when found in the pocket, is often, usually indeed, reverently placed round the dead man's neck before he is wrapped in his blanket for burial. " I put his beads about his neck, sir," is the report often given by the stretcher-bearer to the chaplain or other officer, as a man is given to the grave. How many Catholic soldiers lie in their lonely graves to-day in the war zone with their beads about their necks! How very,

IN THE DARKENED CHURCH

very many! And so, indeed, one feels sure, would they wish to be buried.

In all the horrid welter of war, beyond all doubt the steady and simple faith of the Catholic soldier supplies at least one bright spot that shines and cheers amidst the ruin and devastation all about. And of all the symbols of his faith the soldier's Rosary is foremost.

The fortitude the men seem to draw from their faith is great and marked. The man who has been with his chaplain and who has prepared himself by the Sacraments is ready for any fate, and shows it in his very demeanour. Often the writer has heard officers declare their pleasure at the devotion of the men to their religion, and frequently these officers have been of other religions themselves. A high General Officer once declared that good chaplains are as necessary as good Commanding Officers. The good chaplains are undoubtedly at the

TRENCH PICTURES

front to-day, and they are the first to bear testimony to the goodness of the men.

Both Catholic priests and Catholic soldiers are playing a brave part in the war to-day, and their record, when it comes to be set down, will be one of which the Catholic world may be most justly proud. What the priest does for the Catholic, other ministers do for the men of other creeds. The "Padres" of all denominations may be truly called the prop and comfort of the Army at the front.

VIII

THE FROZEN FRONT LINE

VIII

THE FROZEN FRONT LINE

(February 17, 1917)

As people hurry along to gain the comfort of home fires, do they ever cast even a single thought towards those who in this winter have no home save the trench, where they are exposed under the starlit sky to the full biting force of twenty or twenty-five degrees of frost ?

If the severe cold has been felt in London, where there is at least some measure of shelter and warmth for most people, what must be the experience of those who have to face the rigours of this unusual weather in the open air, not by day alone, but through the night as well?

Each season presents its special difficulties to the men who hold the line. In summer the flies are a veritable plague, and the mud in rainy weather is an everlasting source of inconvenience, to say the least. It is, however, in the depth of winter that the test of endurance is most stringently applied to the men at the front. To say they stand the test well is to understate the case. Nothing could be more magnificent than the glorious way in which our troops face, endure, and triumph over the severity of winter conditions.

Imagine a body of men marching through the snow up to the trenches when a frost of twenty-five degrees prevails. Everything they pass is frozen hard. The village street is deserted, save for the troops engaged on work.

THE FROZEN FRONT LINE

The few remaining villagers stay indoors cowering over their stoves, and only move to the windows to look out at the men who march past on their way to the line. It is so cold out of doors that it is almost impossible to bear the sting of the wind upon one's face. But the boys who are for the trenches swing along, doggedly it may be, but cheerily withal.

On they go. Past the church upon which the snow lies thick, past the graveyard, where all the mounds are covered with spotless palls of white, and where the little memorial crosses glitter with the frost and ice; on past the village street, on and out into the open country march the boys who are for the line. Their pipers are at their head, but it is almost impossible to play, so intense is the cold. On and on they march through the countryside, and now at length they reach the cross-road near which is

TRENCH PICTURES

the entrance to the long communication trench leading to the front line.

Into this trench the men go, and in single file trudge along to their destination—the very front. As they enter the trench and disappear it has an uncanny effect. It is as though the snow had swallowed them up. For the rest of their journey they are shadowed mostly by the trench.

When you who read these lines turn to a warm bed at night, let your mind travel to the line, and picture if you can the men who are defending you in your home—the men who through the long hours of the night, in the frost and snow, stand, under the blazing stars, on the fire-step, peering with never-flagging attention out over the sandbags towards the enemy.

In some trenches the dug-outs are very few, and the merest shelters of sandbag and board and iron sheet are all the pro-

THE FROZEN FRONT LINE

tection the men have. At night, even where there are dug-outs, the alert watch over the parapet must be kept up from the fire-step. Vigilance can never be relaxed. Every sign, every move, every shadow in No Man's Land must be regarded closely. One never knows when an attack may come—nothing can be left to chance.

And so from dusk till daylight the fire-step is manned with ever-ready sentries. Think of what that means all night long, with anything from twenty to thirty degrees of frost; or in pelting, blinding snow, rain, or sleet!

It takes men to hold the long line under these winter conditions; and the amazing thing is that these particular men, in very many cases never were inured to hardships before.

Men who worked in offices, men who knew the good comforts of home life, men who were always protected from

TRENCH PICTURES

cold and damp—men of all sorts who had but little experience of rough conditions—these are the men who, new to soldiering as they are, hold the long line this bitter winter. A marvellous and wonderful achievement when one realises it all, and remembers that the Army is a new Army almost from top to bottom.

And if the men are marvellous, the officers indeed are no less.

Little more than schoolboys, thousands of them—just boys, with all the spirit and joy of life of youth—straight, many of them, from schools and homes of luxury even. And there they are to-night, patrolling the frozen trenches, heartening their men, and proving, in spite of cold and snow and mud and hardship, that there is in their veins blood which will keep on "telling" all the time.

War is a hard and cruel school, but

THE FROZEN FRONT LINE

harder and more cruel surely in the winter time. For some time past the portion of the Western front with which the writer is familiar has been covered with a mantle of pure white snow. Snow on the huts, snow on the guns, snow on the wagons, snow everywhere, on friend and on enemy alike. And through the snow it all goes on—the raid, the bombing, the artillery duel, and all the ugly turmoil of war.

It is of the men, however—the glorious men who in all the hard bitterness of recent weather hold the frozen line by night and day—we should think as the wind blows and drives those who stay at home to the side of their comfortable fires. There is one consoling thought the people at home may have—so far the men who hold the line have been as well fed as, and better probably than, any army ever in the field. That they shall continue to be, should be the very first

TRENCH PICTURES

care of every one in the homeland. Whatever grumbling there may be at economies at home, should cease for ever at the mere thought of what is being done by the men in the Frozen Front Line.

IX

RELIGION AND THE WAR

IX

RELIGION AND THE WAR

(February 26, 1917)

WITH all the evil that has followed in its train it is good to find at least one beneficial result from the war. It has led to the revival of religion in a most remarkable way.

As to this, practically every one is agreed, and it is apparent in a hundred directions. Perhaps this revival is most marked of all in France, and there it is attributable in no little degree to the splendid record of the French priests in the Army.

To many people it seemed a wrong thing that the ministers of the Prince of

TRENCH PICTURES

Peace should be called upon to take up arms, and play a part in the terrible work of bloodshed and slaughter which has converted so large a portion of Europe into a veritable shambles. What seemed wrong, and what from some points of view was wrong no doubt, has in the result turned out a blessing.

The spectacle of thousands of priests marching and fighting for the country and the flag has touched deeply the heart of France, and many and many a man who was, perhaps, ready enough to proclaim himself an anti-Cleric will never so describe himself any more. The bravery displayed by the French priests in battle (2,000 have been killed) has been only equalled by their devotion to their holy office.

Few things are more appealing than the sight of the soldier-priest turning to administer the last consolations of religion to his fallen comrades round about.

RELIGION AND THE WAR

And this has been witnessed on every battlefield of France. It has its natural effect upon the impressionable French character, and that effect will remain long after the last shot of the war has been fired.

To those who have been brought to France by the war, the manifestations of religion everywhere displayed have come more or less as a surprise, especially to those who had been led to believe from the action of many successive French Governments that the Church was more or less a thing of the past in France.

It is hard, of course, to judge of the real depth or intensity of religious feeling, but all one can say is, that if this can be judged by noticing the attendance at church, then the religion of France is to-day very true and very sincere.

For over a year the writer of these lines has been with the British Army in France, and has been billeted in scores of villages and small towns. Everywhere the way in which the civil population thronged the churches on Sundays and holidays was very noticeable, and in the larger towns more noticeable still.

It may be that the attacks which the enemy have made on holy places have caused a revulsion of feeling in France. The ruins of Rheims Cathedral, Ypres, and so many other churches in the land have stricken the population with remorse and sorrow.

Certain it is, be the real reason what it may, there has been a great revival in the devoutness of the French people since war broke out. Of course the cynical will say, " The devil was sick, the devil a saint would be," etc., but the change goes deeper than this.

The Faith has ever been firmly and deeply planted in the French heart, and it needed but the tribulation of suffering and war to make the people see clearly the value of that which is, after all, in the time of trouble the only real bulwark and consolation for humanity. And so it has been, that through the smoke of battle the light of Faith has flamed out once more brightly throughout France, and the faces of the people are gladly turned towards it.

The writer has seen more deep and reverent devotion displayed by worshippers inside the walls of semi-ruined churches which had their stained-glass windows shattered, than ever he has seen before. Probably more fervent prayers have been poured out before broken crosses and shell-torn statues of our Saviour in France and Belgium than were ever offered in peace time before the most beautiful shrines in the whole world.

By accident or design—one must decide according to the measure of one's charity—the Germans have destroyed many churches and shrines and convents in the war. They present a sad spectacle indeed, but it would seem that in proportion to the ruin thus caused, the Faith has taken refuge more and more in the hearts of the people, with the result that, in the opinion of most men, Religion has been perhaps the one thing in all the world, so far, strengthened and built up afresh amidst the horrible ravages of war. That there has been a similar result all over the world, and away from the actual scene of war, is the testimony of unbiassed observers.

The fact is that the ruin and carnage have been so stupendous, the sacrifices have been so great, the horrors have been so widespread, and have so penetrated into almost every family circle, that almost every human being in the world has been affected and has turned tó look for hope and comfort beyond the grave. Miserable indeed is the man or woman

RELIGION AND THE WAR

who is not assured that that hope and comfort is so to be found; for, in sooth, this war has made this transitory world but a sorry place.

The writer of these impressions has been with a section of the British Army in the field, which numbers very many Catholic soldiers in its ranks. The conduct of these men has undoubtedly had a good effect upon the population, wherever they have been stationed. The majority of the soldiers are of Irish nationality, though of English and Scottish and Overseas Catholic soldiers there are also not a few. The simple and yet deep faith exhibited by these men upon all occasions made a wonderful impression on the French and Belgian peoples.

It is not at the very best a happy thing to have one's country occupied by foreign troops, even though they come to defend your soil from the invader.

TRENCH PICTURES

Masses of men overrunning villages and towns, and eager for some sort of relaxation from the rigour and hardship of trench life, are apt to give trouble, even though well behaved and well disposed in every way.

It is always a source of anxiety to the higher command to secure that nothing, even by inadvertence, shall be done by the troops to cause annoyance to the inhabitants of occupied territory. The outstanding feature of the British occupation of France and Belgium has been the fine and chivalrous spirit displayed by the men. They have put themselves on a footing of the best and kindest sort with the people, and complaints of any kind as to their behaviour are few and far between.

But, in addition to the relief of the people in finding the troops kind and considerate, imagine the good impression created when the French people find that

RELIGION AND THE WAR

large numbers of the men are devoted to their own religion and most earnest in their practice of it.

When Irish regiments are billeted in a village, the church, large enough for the villagers, becomes at once too small. It is thronged by the soldiers, and the curé finds his congregation enormous, and has, in conjunction with the Army chaplains, to arrange for many services on Sunday.

The General commanding a division composed for the most part of Irish Catholic soldiers, informed the present writer that his division never left an area without the local authorities, and notably the curé, coming to him to express their appreciation of the good behaviour of the troops, and their admiration for their earnest devotion to their religion.

There is no doubt that the scourge of war has purified the hearts of many people, and the advent of large numbers of Catholic troops into France has probably helped to bring back to some Frenchmen an appreciation of something which they at one time seemed almost to have lost. Thus in one way, and a way of no little importance, the war has wrought a change for the better in France.

X

THE SQUARE OF EMPIRE

X

THE SQUARE OF EMPIRE

(April 14, 1917)

THERE is a fair-sized French town some distance from the firing line which is much frequented by British officers. They go there to visit the field cashier and to draw money to pay the men; they go there to buy stores at the Expeditionary Force canteen; and sometimes, when duty permits, they visit the town to spend an hour at the officers' club or to take tea at the officers' tea rooms in the Grande Place, where the town hall is on one side, and the church on the other.

The Grande Place, or the Square as

TRENCH PICTURES

the men call it, is the great meeting-place for visitors to the town. In the centre, the mess carts which have come in for supplies wait drawn up in a line whilst the shopping is being done; and in and out of the stores on each side officers of many different units are encountered, busy upon all the little errands which are entrusted to them by comrades who are not lucky enough to be able to enjoy a few hours' relaxation from the monotony of trench and camp, in the town. The officers' tea room is a favourite rendezvous.

And a cheery spot it is, bedecked with the flags of the Allied nations. All the appointments of the place are good—clean cloths upon the little tea tables, little bunches of flowers here and there, and altogether an air of brightness and comfort about, very grateful indeed to eyes weary of the drab dismalness of trench and hut.

THE SQUARE OF EMPIRE

In the hours of the afternoon the tea room is crowded with officers from various units, and it is of interest to observe that they represent very often branches of the Army in the field from almost every corner of the Empire.

This fact was specially noticeable one afternoon when the writer visited the tea room with a friend. At a table in one corner sat a grey-headed major, wearing a Canadian badge, eating pastry with all the earnestness and attention which a small schoolboy might have bestowed upon that operation.

In another corner a party of Australian officers were appreciating the tea, and talking of the times when they were wont to brew their own tea in billy-cans on a certain sheep-run in sunny New South Wales. Not far away some other officers sat—Scottish clearly—alike by their tongues and by their bare strong knees.

TRENCH PICTURES

And so all through the room, officers—English, Irish, Scottish, and Welsh, and Overseas—were seated, representing almost all parts of the world-wide Empire of Britain, and constituting, so to speak, an informal but very cheery Imperial military conference at tea.

In the square outside the tea room the representation of the Empire was even more complete. The town the writer speaks of is a centre where converged from time to time officers and men from several divisions, and so there is an opportunity almost any afternoon of encountering men from every part, even the most distant, of the Empire.

One evening, just before dusk, the writer was passing through the square, which was covered with snow. A party of tall soldiers were engaged making a passage through, shovelling the snow away. They were Australians. Ques-

THE SQUARE OF EMPIRE

tioned as to whether they felt the cold very severely, one great, tall fellow replied : " My word ! I should say so ! But it is all new and interesting to me, for I have never seen snow before ! I come, you see, from Queensland, and the north of that!" Indeed, it seemed there were men in this snow-clearing party from Tasmania and all over Australia, from Brisbane to Perth and from the Northern Territory to Adelaide.

Passing to another portion of the square, some New Zealand troops were to be seen marching along from the railway station. They too, like their Australian comrades, were fine upstanding fellows, and they made nothing of the bitter cold and biting wind. There is something free and dashing in the gait and appearance of these Australians and New Zealanders which seems to attract the French. Certain it is that wherever these great Overseas

TRENCH PICTURES

fellows go, with their broad-brimmed soft hats jauntily set upon their heads, they invariably are the object of much friendly attention from the French population of the towns and villages through which they pass.

There is nothing more remarkable than the way in which these men, reared and brought up in hot and sunny lands, have settled down to the life at the front, where for quite a considerable time almost Arctic conditions have prevailed. To the Canadians—and they were also to be met with in the same square—the wintry conditions were no inconvenience; indeed, the prevailing weather reminded them of home.

Men from a South African brigade were also to be seen going by, and it was a not unusual sight to see the little groups up and down the square composed of Australians, Canadians, New Zealanders, and Africans, all together, chatting over that favourite topic, the probable duration of the war, and comparing notes as to their various and widely sundered homes.

Sometimes one encountered Indian troops in the square, but latterly Indian troops are not stationed in this district; and mingling with all these splendid troops from the most remote portions of the Empire one met representatives from units brought together from John o' Groat's to Land's End: Welshmen and Scotsmen, too, and Englishmen from every city and shire.

Just as the companion of the writer of these lines was remarking that we had in one brief hour met with troops representing the whole Imperial Army save Ireland, a couple of men passed, and, as if to complete the picture, they turned out to be, as their shamrock badges clearly indicated, Munster Fusiliers. Very tired they seemed, carrying their full equipment, and probably returning from leave, for they came from the direction of the railway station. Presently a G.S. wagon came along bearing on its side the Ulster badge of the Red Hand. The Munster soldiers hailed the wagon as it passed. "Can you give us a lift along the road?" Promptly the answer came, "Righto! In ye get, my shamrock boys!"

And so, as if to emphasise the United Imperial experience encountered in the square, the spectacle was witnessed of these men of the North and South proceeding on their way in brotherhood, and exchanging as they went that special kind of cigarette dear to the soldier's heart and rejoicing in the doubtful description of "Gasper!"

A truly wonderful place, this old square in the French town, where one may meet men from all over the world-wide Empire, and where Australian and Canadian,

THE SQUARE OF EMPIRE

South African and New Zealander, mingle with the men of the homelands, all bound together by a common sentiment and all having in view a common object.

XI

IN "NO MAN'S LAND"

XI

IN "NO MAN'S LAND"

(April 1, 1916)

SUNDAY morning. The mist rose lazily from around the trench as the dawn broke. For more than a week the weather had been vile. Snow and sleet, rain and fog. The men in the trench had been "fed up" with it. Their clothes were damp through and through, and they found it next to impossible to keep their rifles free from rust. They had given up all efforts to keep even a little of the mud off. It lapped itself about them everywhere—and they were "fed up" with it.

But with the dawning of Sunday there

was a change. The fog disappeared. The sky, lowering and dark for so long, turned into an expanse of purest blue. A lark, rising from God knows where on that dismal war-seared plain, rose high over the trench and sang, and sang, and sang blithely. The screaming of the shells, the roar of the guns seemed silenced by the song. The men looked up and listened, pausing in their work, pausing even in taking their hasty meal. It was a wonderful song. The trench-stained men were transported by it. They were no longer amidst ruin and misery and war. The song brought them back to their homes, and they stood in the pleasant fields of Ireland, and listened as they had so often done to the skylark on high.

For a long time no word was spoken; it seemed as though the men feared that even a whisper might stay the song. So they just looked at the tiny hovering

IN "NO MAN'S LAND"

speck in the blue sky, and listened. Then suddenly the bird sank down to the rough, shell-ploughed earth, as if satisfied with having sung its Sunday message over the trench.

Then Murphy spoke. A big rough fellow to look at, but " with a heart in him," as is sometimes said. " Faith, that's a great little bird." The other men said, " Aye, so it is," and went about their work. Later on a man who had been looking into the little periscope on his bayonet turned, and said excitedly, " The spring is here—the grass is growing out there like anything ! " And they all peeped over the parapet.

It was true. In the bleak and rough stretch of ground, called " No Man's Land," between their own wire entanglements and the enemy's, the grass, in spite of all, was springing " fresh and green." It sprang up around old bully-beef tins and old jam tins. It sprang up and nestled around an old broken bayonet, and grew about, as though it meant to cover it, an empty shell-case. The men suddenly seemed to realise that, in spite of all the death and desolation and the ruined walls of the town near by, there was new life and hope in the air and all about, a life that even great guns could never destroy—the life of God.

It was wonderful and pathetic, too, how these Irishmen were cheered by the simple discovery that spring had come and the grass was sprouting. A few forlorn trees behind the trench, their topmost branches broken and jagged by shot, were also budding, " in spite," as Private Kelly said, " of even the divil himself! " The snow, the rain, the damp clothes, the mud—everything miserable seemed to be forgotten in the trench that Sunday morning, and the men whistled and said, as they

IN "NO MAN'S LAND"

looked up into the blue overhead, "Glory be to God! It's a grand spring day!"

Later on some enemy battle-planes winged their way high over the line, accompanied by the little white puffs of smoke from the shells which were fired at them, and which hung in the blue sky like little balls of wool. Enemy aeroplanes were common sights enough —the men did not trouble to look at them as much as they had looked at the skylark. Spring had come to the trench, and with it renewed hope and courage and heart to everybody.

The change was wonderful, and surely never were the budding of a tree and the springing of grass so welcomed as in that desolate place. The men hummed Army popular songs as they rested on the firestep or busied themselves at the neverending work of improving their trench. From the far side of the traverse came the sizzling sound of frying, and a jolly voice chanted.

> I see you there, Isabel!
> I see you there very well.
> I am frying bacon, Isabel,
> As you can tell—very well—
> By the smell—Isabel!

The growing of the grass on "No Man's Land" cheered every one up, and the men said to each other with meaning, "Some day it won't be always 'No Man's Land'!" Later that Sunday the priest came to the trench, and the Irishmen stood around bareheaded as he spoke to them and asked them to pray for dead comrades, and to prepare themselves to die, if die they must. And then he gave them Absolution. The men very earnestly listened, and repeated in many Irish accents, both North and South, the prayer the good priest said. It was a rough surrounding from which to worship the Almighty, but overhead the

IN "NO MAN'S LAND"

blue vault of heaven was finer than any cathedral dome; and what choir could touch the lark which, hovering high between heaven and earth, sang while the men prayed?

XII

"JACK," THE PET DOG

XII

"JACK," THE PET DOG

WHEN he exactly arrived, or from where, nobody seemed to know. We were all agreed, however, that he was a very smart-looking little fox-terrier —well bred and well marked. He had probably belonged to some officer and had got lost. The battalion first made his acquaintance one morning as the men were drawn up in column of fours waiting to march off to the next village to new billets. Jack—as he was promptly christened—trotted out of an estaminet, and, seeing the battalion drawn up, sat down on his tail and calmly surveyed what was going on in the street.

TRENCH PICTURES

The men took a fancy to Jack at once, and whistled and shouted at him. The dog got up and gravely strolled along as though he had made up his mind to inspect the men. He went to the front of the column and looked at the colonel, and surveyed the band. He went to the rear of the column and made the acquaintance of the second-in-command, and then, as if he had thoroughly made up his mind, he attached himself to "B" Company. This choice he probably made because Company Sergeant-Major of B Company had stooped down, and, patting him, cheerfully said, "Hello, Jack, and how are *you* to-day?" Of course nobody really knew the little dog's name, but when Sergeant Brady called him Jack, Jack he remained until he finally disappeared in the mist and smoke of one terrible day on the Somme.

From the date of his arrival Jack

"JACK," THE PET DOG

never left the battalion, nor, indeed, B Company. After a while he was provided with a collar, bright green in colour. If ever there was a pure-bred English fox-terrier, Jack undoubtedly was one; but having joined, so to speak, an Irish battalion, he graciously submitted to the green collar, though, indeed, it was as often as not covered with the mud through which he cheerfully trotted as his company marched along. The company sergeant-major and the little dog became fast friends; though Jack, being probably an old soldier, thoroughly understood the advantage of being on good terms also with the company quartermaster, whose store he promptly made the acquaintance of in every village where the battalion found billets.

It was extraordinary how the presence of this little animal cheered up the men. He never missed a parade, and even early on the cold and bitter mornings Jack was always present, always cheery and "merry and bright," as the men used to remark. Wherever Jack was met with it might be assumed that the company sergeant-major was not far off. Just as we read in the *Cricket on the Hearth*, that whenever people met the carrier's dog, Boxer, on the road, they always looked out for John Pereybingle himself; so, whenever any one saw Jack trotting round the street of a village, somewhere in France, it became a certainty that Sergeant Brady was close at hand. Just too as Boxer used to drop into houses along the road, so Jack did the same, always with an air, however, of friendly politeness, as of one who should say to the inmates, "There are a lot of Irish soldiers coming along, but you need not mind them; they are good

"JACK," THE PET DOG

fellows all, and you should come out and hear the pipes!"

Sometimes the battalion returned to the same villages, and then Jack was hailed as an old friend by lots of the inhabitants. In marching through the streets of some considerable town, Jack and his green collar gained quite as much attention as the stately regimental sergeant-major, or even the colonel himself at the head of the battalion, and many were the exclamations of interest and admiration showered upon him, particularly by the children, as he trotted along. The little chap never seemed to tire, even on the longest march, and he always found time to get off the road and scamper through the fields at each side with a business-like air, as much as to say, "If there *is* a rabbit to be had, it might come in handy."

Once, when the battalion was drawn

up ready to march out of the village, Jack was not to be found, and it is no exaggeration to say that there was consternation in the company. When the captain came out to inspect his men prior to marching off, it was with a real note of trouble in his voice that the sergeant, after announcing "all present," declared that Jack was not to be discovered. Then the captain exhibited signs of trouble too, and ordered a search to be made in the billets. Later on, after he had been released from an old stable, the door of which had been inadvertently closed upon him, Master Jack was received with acclamation; and, having jumped upon the sergeant by way of explaining his absence and apologising for it, he scampered off according to custom to have a word with the colonel, see the band, and then back, so that the second-in-command in the rear might know

"JACK," THE PET DOG

that, as far as he, Jack, was concerned, everything was all right!

The battalion's days of billeting in French villages and walking along country roads soon came to an end, and the grim life in the trenches commenced. Jack went to the trenches too—always with B Company; and though clearly puzzled by the absence of landscape, the little dog still kept "merry and bright" and followed the sergeant everywhere. Once he got—how, nobody could tell exactly—over the top, and was discovered sitting on a sandbag calmly surveying No Man's Land. He was hurriedly pulled down, and not a moment too soon, for several rifle bullets came thudding unpleasantly close to where he had been.

The rats were his special and particular interest, and from one end of the trench to the other he declared war on them, and many a one he brought

TRENCH PICTURES

in triumph to lay at the feet of his friend the sergeant. The writer of these lines (for, be it understood, this is a true narrative) once asked the sergeant whether he kept Jack with him in his dug-out at night. "Lord bless you, sir! No, sir! Jack has a dug-out of his own! I'll show you, sir." With a smile the sergeant walked along the trench till he came to a great niche or indentation in the side, where rifle ammunition was stored. Two of the boxes had been removed in the centre, and in the hole thus made, with some sand-bags underneath, Jack was discovered comfortably curled up: A quaint and curious picture, making one long for a Kodak; the little dog, with his brown eyes peering out from a bed banked all round with boxes of cartridges! that was his sleeping place by night. When the sergeant went for a little rest, Jack, so to speak, bid him good-

"JACK," THE PET DOG

night and trotted along to his own little nest amidst the explosives! Every morning, however, at " stand-to " Jack was on duty, and usually accompanied the officer who superintended the serving out of tots of rum to the men.

As to meals, Jack bestowed his company impartially. One day he had breakfast with one platoon and the next day with another, but wherever he went he never lacked offers of hospitality, and the men laughed as they noticed that life in the trenches made their little pet fat. The day finally arrived when the battalion marched to the Somme and took part in an advance. Jack was with them to the end; but, like so many of his friends amongst the men, he never returned out of the smoke and turmoil of that terrible day. He was after all, it is true, only a wee little animal,

TRENCH PICTURES

but nevertheless he truly "did his bit," and cheered the men many a day in trench and along the weary road of march. Jack is gone, but there are some men still left who remember him, and any of them would think little or nothing of settling a Hun; but not a single one of them would ever agree that a pet dog should be put to death. That is their tribute to the memory of little Jack!

APPENDIX

MAJOR REDMOND'S LAST SPEECH

Major William Redmond at 54. (Feb. 1915).

APPENDIX

MAJOR REDMOND'S LAST SPEECH IN THE HOUSE OF COMMONS

(March 7, 1917)

I HAVE been asked to second the motion which has just been so ably spoken to by my hon. friend. I promise that, in seconding the motion, I will be extremely brief, and I do not know that I would have taken the opportunity of saying even a few words here this afternoon were it not that I feel I can give some expression to the great volume of opinion which is held by those of my countrymen who are doing their best in the field.

Whatever may have taken place, nothing can alter this fact, that when war was declared large numbers of the Irish people responded to the appeal made to them. They responded readily, and, as I venture to think, gallantly. They responded for many reasons. In the first place, on the broad issue of the war, there

APPENDIX

could be no doubt—there can still be no doubt —the great, generous heart of the Irish race beats in sympathy with the Allies' cause, and no matter what may have happened, no matter what still may happen in the future, nothing can alter my firm conviction that, apart from everything else, the great heart of Ireland, North and South as well, beats in strong sympathy with the gallant efforts which are being made by the French nation to-day to free their soil from the invader.

Nothing can change my conviction that the overwhelming majority of the Irish people have been outraged in all their dearest feelings by what has taken place in Belgium, and I venture to say that the Irish people who did respond, responded also—and this brings me to the subject of my brief remarks this afternoon—because they were led to believe that a new and a better and brighter chapter was about to open in the relations of Great Britain and Ireland.

I ask you, Mr. Speaker, and I ask the members of this house, irrespective of parties, to realise, if they possibly can, the feelings of men who went out, impelled by that motive, when they hear vague rumours from time to time that their response to the appeal of this

MAJOR REDMOND'S LAST SPEECH

country has been more or less in vain, and that what they hope for is not, after all, to be accomplished.

A man who, in the trying circumstances which surround life abroad, has those feelings, is surely to be considered and commiserated. And I know that if anything could tend towards strengthening the resolve which is still strong in the Irish troops to do their duty, it would be the feeling that a better and a newer chapter with Great Britain was about to be opened, and that their country was about to be trusted with the rights and freedom of self-government.

My hon. friend who has just resumed his seat spoke with all his wonted eloquence of many sad things in the past. It is easy enough, God knows, to talk about the past. In regard to Ireland it is not always pleasant. The past is a thing which can be enlarged upon for any length of time, but I venture to think, at this time of day, with very little profit. I do not believe that there is a single member of any party in this house who is prepared to get up and say that in the past the government and treatment of Ireland by Great Britain have been what they should have been.

Mistakes—dark, black, and bitter mistakes

APPENDIX

—have been made. A people denied justice, a people with many admitted grievances, the redress of which has been long delayed ; on our side, perhaps, in the conflict, and in the bitterness of contest, there may have been things said and done, offensive if you will, irritating if you will, to the people of this country ; but what I want to ask, in all simplicity, is this, whether, in face of the tremendous conflict which is now raging, whether, in view of the fact that, apart from every other consideration, the Irish people, South as well as North, are upon the side of the Allies and against the German pretension to-day, it is not possible from this war to make a new start ; whether it is not possible on your side, and on ours as well, to let the dead past bury its dead, and to commence a brighter and a newer and a friendlier era between the two countries ?

Why cannot we do it ? Is there an Englishman representing any party who does not yearn for a better future between Ireland and Great Britain ? There is no Irishman who is not anxious for it also. Why cannot there be a settlement ? Why must it be that, when British soldiers and Irish soldiers are suffering and dying side by side, this eternal old quarrel should go on ?

MAJOR REDMOND'S LAST SPEECH

It is not, after all, an English and an Irish question. It is not, after all, a question merely affecting the Empire. It is a question affecting the whole world. There is not a corner of the civilised world to-day where the Irish question does not exercise influence, and you see in the public press every morning the efforts which are being made by our enemies to exploit the position of Ireland.

Canada everybody is proud of. Australia has done her part splendidly in this struggle. Why cannot you listen to them ? Canada five times in her Parliament has begged you to deal with the Irish question on broad and free lines, and Australia has done the same. In God's name, why cannot you do it ? I do not believe there is an Englishman in Europe who would not this very night agree to a full and free measure of Home Rule if the Irish people themselves would demand it.

What stands in the way of a settlement ? The attitude of a section of our countrymen in the North of Ireland ! If you ask an Englishman, be he Liberal or Conservative, why Home Rule is not granted, the reply will be, "Home Rule we are ready to grant—every journal in England says so—if only you and your countrymen, North and South, can agree about it."

APPENDIX

If there ought to be an oblivion of the past between Great Britain and Ireland generally, may I ask in God's name the First Lord of the Admiralty why there cannot be a similar oblivion of the past between the warring sections in Ireland?

Are we to ever go on the lines of the old struggle of the Stuarts and the Battle of the Boyne? All my life I have taken as strong and as strenuous a part on the Nationalist side as my poor abilities would allow. I may have been as bitter and as strong in the heated atmosphere of party contests against my countrymen in the North as ever they have been against me, but I believe in my soul and heart here to-day that I represent the instinct and the desire of the whole Irish Catholic race when I say that there is nothing that they more passionately desire and long for than that there should be an end of this old struggle between the North and the South.

The followers of the right hon. gentleman the First Lord of the Admiralty should shake hands with the rest of their countrymen. I appeal to the right hon. gentleman here in the name of men against whom no finger of scorn can be pointed; in the name of men who are doing their duty; in the name of men who

MAJOR REDMOND'S LAST SPEECH

have died ; in the name of men who may die, and who at this very moment may be dying, to rise to the demands of the situation. I ask him to meet his Nationalist fellow-countrymen and accept the offer which they make to him and his followers, and on the basis of that self-government which has made, and which alone has made, the Empire as strong as it is to-day, come to some arrangement for the better government of Ireland in the future.

What stands in the way ? We read in our history books of the Battle of the Boyne. The friends of the right hon. gentleman espoused the cause of William hundreds of years ago. Our people passionately adhere to the cause of the fallen Stuarts. Is the sentiment engendered at that time to go on for ever ? In the face of a war which is threatening civilisation, which is destroying all that mankind has built up in the Christian era, in the face of all that, are we still to continue in Ireland our conflicts and our arguments and disputes about the merits of the Stuarts, about the Battle of the Boyne and the rest ?

Why does the right hon. gentleman opposite not meet us half-way ? I want to know what is the reason. It surely cannot be that the right hon. gentleman and his friends believe

APPENDIX

that under a system of self-government they would have anything to fear. Nothing impressed me more than the opinion I heard expressed by a high-placed Roman Catholic officer who is in service with the Ulster Brigade, than when he told me of his experience there, and when he said that although he was the only one of the Catholic religion in that division it had dawned upon him that they certainly were Irishmen and were not Englishmen or Scotsmen.

The right hon. gentleman knows perfectly well that it would not take so very much to bring his friends and our friends together, and I ask him why the attempt is not made. I ask him whether the circumstances of the time do not warrant that such an attempt should be made ? I ask him whether he does not know in his inmost heart that it would bring to the common enemy more dismay and consternation than the destruction of a hundred of their submarines if they knew that England, Scotland, and Ireland were really united, not merely within the confines of the shores of these islands, but united in every part of the world where the Irish people are to be found ?

The right hon. gentleman may ask for guarantees or safeguards in an Irish Par-

MAJOR REDMOND'S LAST SPEECH

liament. My own opinion is that those he represents desire in their hearts no guarantees or safeguards. I believe that they know that they can trust their countrymen in the South. Does anybody believe that the southern Irish heart is capable of anything which would be other than upright and just and fair to the people of the North in the legislative chamber ? Does anybody think them capable of such baseness ? What is it that stands in the way of Ireland taking her place as a self-governing part of this Empire ?

Ireland is the only portion of the Empire now fighting which is not self-governing. The Australians whom I meet from time to time point to their government being free ; the Canadians and the New Zealanders do the same, and we Irishmen are the only units in France to-day taking our part in the war who are obliged to admit that the country we come from is denied those privileges which has made the Empire the strong organisation which it is to-day.

If safeguards are necessary—I speak only for myself, and I do not speak for anybody else on these benches, because I have been away from this house so long that I have almost lost touch with things—as far as my

APPENDIX

own personal opinion goes, there is nothing I would not do, and there is no length to which I would not go, in order to meet the real objections or to secure the real confidence, friendship, and affection of my countrymen in the North of Ireland.

For my own part, I would gladly, if it would ease the situation, agree to an arrangement whereby it might be possible for His Majesty the King, if he so desired, to call in some one at the starting of a new Irish government, a gentleman representing the portion of the country and the section of the community which the First Lord represents, and if a representative of that kind were placed with his hand upon the helm of the first Irish Parliament, I—at any rate, as far as I am concerned—would give him the loyal and the strong support which I have given to every leader I have supported in this house.

After all, these are times of sacrifice, and every man is called upon to make some sacrifices. Men and women and children alike have to do something in these days, and is it too much to appeal to the right hon. gentleman and his friends to sacrifice some part of their position in order to lead the majority of their countrymen and to bring about that

MAJOR REDMOND'S LAST SPEECH

which the whole English-speaking world desires, namely, a real reconciliation of Ireland?

I apologise for having detained the house so long, but this is a matter upon which I feel strongly, and I feel all the more strongly about it because I know that I am trying altogether too feebly, but as strongly as I can, to represent what I know to be the wishes nearest to the hearts of tens of thousands of Irishmen who went with me and their colleagues to France, many of whom will never return, all of whom are suffering the privations and the hardship and the risk and the wellnigh intolerable circumstances of life in France.

I want to speak for these men, and if they could all speak with one voice and with one accord they would say to this house, to men in every part of it, to Conservatives, Liberals, and Labour men, to their Nationalist countrymen and to their countrymen from the North of Ireland, in the name of God we here who are about to die, perhaps, ask you to do that which largely induced us to leave our homes; to do that which our fathers and mothers taught us to long for; to do that which is all we desire, make our country happy and contented, and enable us when we meet the Canadians and the Australians and the New

APPENDIX

Zealanders, side by side in the common cause and the common field, to say to them, " Our country, just as yours, has self-government within the Empire."

I know that there is a great softening of feeling with regard to Ireland. I know there is not the same bitterness which there used to be. I know that men of all parties recognise that there is an Irish question. How well I remember, when I came in here as a boy nearly thirty-four years ago, that people used to say, " Oh, the curse of Ireland is the agitator, and but for the agitator Ireland would be at rest and peace."

Never, surely, was there a greater fallacy than that. It is not the agitator that makes the agitation in Ireland or anywhere else ; it is the unrest amongst the people, and their discontent, which make the agitators. For thirty-four years I have been begging the people of this country here to prepare for the danger which now confronts them, by trusting Ireland.

For many years my own father on this very bench preached the same thing, and pleaded the same cause, and if nothing is done, when we are all dead and gone, and the whole personnel of this house is changed, when a new generation arises to which all that is now hap-

MAJOR REDMOND'S LAST SPEECH

pening will be but a mere matter of history, there will then be still the Irish question, which is simply the result of attempting to govern a high-spirited people against their consent, and without reference to their individual and instinctive feelings.

Therefore it is that at the risk of wearying the house I have made these remarks, and I do appeal with all the strength of my soul to the Government, to its Leader, and to the First Lord of the Admiralty, to seize the opportunity which has now arisen. It cannot be beyond the wit of men to reconcile the differences of the past. In view of the extraordinary necessities of the time, it surely ought to be the duty of Ulstermen and Nationalists alike to meet each other, and to bring about in Ireland a state of affairs which will rejoice the Empire, and which will bring satisfaction from one end of the United States of America and the English-speaking world to the other.

www.ingramcontent.com/pod-product-compliance
Lightning Source LLC
Chambersburg PA
CBHW031955080426
42735CB00007B/400